INSPIRATIONAL QUOTATIONS

splash!

refreshing motivational quotes
to sip, savor, and share

SUSAN ROHRER

Devotional Reflections for Spirit-Filled Christian Living

Infinite
Arts
Media

SPLASH! INSPIRATIONAL QUOTATIONS:
Refreshing Motivational Quotes to Sip, Savor, and Share
(Devotional Reflections for Spirit-Filled Christian Living Series)

Written by Susan Rohrer

Kindly direct inquiries about novel or screenplay to:
InfiniteArtsMgmt@gmail.com

Readers may follow or message author at:

www.twitter.com/suroar
www.pinterest.com/IAMsusanrohrer

Permission to share, tweet, or otherwise briefly quote this book on non-commercial venues such as social networking websites or blogs is hereby freely granted to all bona fide purchasers of this book under the following conditions:

Excerpts must be quoted exactly as written;
Limited to one brief quote per single post;
All quotes must be attributed to Susan Rohrer.

Excepting brief excerpts for review purposes and singular quotes for brief non-commercial sharing and tweeting as specified above, no part of this book may be reproduced or used in any form without written permission from the author.

This book includes quotations from the author's following books under separate copyright:

The Holy Spirit—Spiritual Gifts: Amazing Power for Everyday People
Is God Saying He's The One?: Relationship Advice for Single Christian Women
Bridle My Heart: A Western Love Story
Secrets of the Dry Bones: The Mystery of a Prophet's Vision

All Scripture quotations taken from the New American Standard Bible®, Copyright © 1960, 1962, 1963, 1968, 1971, 1972, 1973, 1975, 1977, 1995 by The Lockman Foundation, used by permission. (www.Lockman.org)

Except as referenced from Scripture, these quotes are original to the author of this book. Any resemblance to quotes from other authors or persons living or dead is entirely coincidental and beyond the intent of the author or publisher.

All Images: Courtesy of morgueFile
Author Photo: Jean-Louis Darville

ISBN-13: 978-151192035
ISBN-10: 1511929030

©Copyright 2015, 2018, Susan Rohrer, all rights reserved.

1 2 3 4 5 6 7 8 9 10 11 12 13 14 15

Published in the United States of America

First Edition 2015

To the Fountain of Living Waters
from whom true refreshment flows

contents

preface — 9

river words — 11
Reflections on Spirit-filled Living

cool waters — 31
Refreshing Currents

liquid love — 47
Awash in Adoration

thirst quenchers — 55
Hydration for Dry Days

swimming single — 69
Lifelines for Spouse Seekers

afterword — 79

about the author — 83

preface

Are you a busy believer? Barely have time to splash some water on your face before you start the day?

You may find yourself thirsty for time with God. You long for a refreshing from the Holy Spirit, an inspired thought for the day ahead. You desire to drink of the living waters Jesus said would flow from the innermost parts of every believer. You want to refresh others with what refreshes you.

Draw from the well of inspiration through this collection of Christian quotes excerpted from what's been poured out in the life of this author. This book is not meant to replace or take priority over quiet time spent in prayer and reading the Bible. Still, we hope you'll be blessed by this fruit of another believer's time spent soaking in the current of God's river.

Whether you're looking for a quick bit of godly insight, a Spirit-filled thought for the day, or something encouraging to share in a post or tweet, you're welcome to draw from these pages. The majority of these quotes have been popular tweets from this author. Thus, there are numerous quotations under 140 characters in length to allow space for attribution. Many of the lengthier quotations were culled from readers' frequently highlighted passages from the author's books. Quotes incorporated with graphics and many more like them can be found and repinned on Pinterest at this link:

www.pinterest.com/IAMSusanRohrer

While most chapters in this book cite quotes that can pertain to anyone regardless of gender or relational circumstance, there's a special chapter at the end with some longer quotes for single women and those who counsel them. So, if you're a solo sister, looking for that special match made in heaven, check out that final chapter intended just for you, entitled *Swimming Single*.

You may wonder why these brief inspirational sayings are called devotional reflections since most can be read so quickly. They're purposely brief to allow you time to reflect upon them. So, take them in and ask God what application each might have to your life. Take a moment to sit quietly and wait for an answer. A Bible verse may come to mind, or perhaps a familiar situation in your life. Respond if the Holy Spirit calls you to action.

Ready to wade into the waters?

Stick a toe in. Drink as deeply as you like. Sip and savor these mini devotionals for your personal edification or share them one-at-a-time with friends and family in need of refreshment.

What are you waiting for?

Jump into the current of God's invigorating river and splash to your heart's delight!

river words

⋈

"They drink their fill of the abundance of Thy house; and Thou dost give them to drink of the river of Thy delights."

Psalm 36:8

⋈

Reflections on Spirit-filled Living

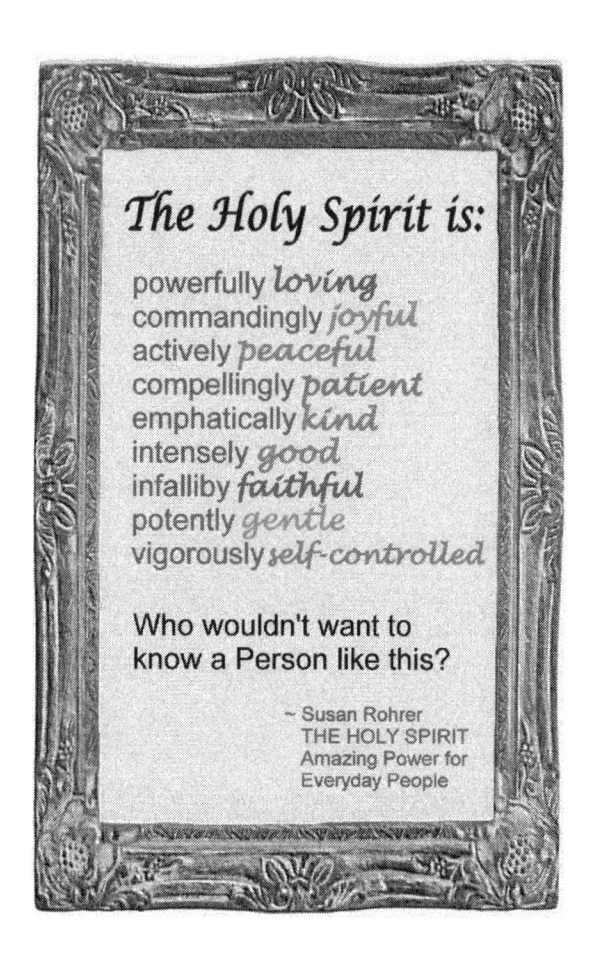

> The Holy Spirit is:
> powerfully *loving*
> commandingly *joyful*
> actively *peaceful*
> compellingly *patient*
> emphatically *kind*
> intensely *good*
> infalliby *faithful*
> potently *gentle*
> vigorously *self-controlled*
>
> Who wouldn't want to know a Person like this?
>
> ~ Susan Rohrer
> THE HOLY SPIRIT
> Amazing Power for
> Everyday People

The Holy Spirit is powerfully loving, commandingly joyful, actively peaceful, compellingly patient, emphatically kind, intensely good, infallibly faithful, potently gentle, and vigorously self-controlled.

Who wouldn't want to know a person like this?

⋈⋈

The Holy Spirit is a great gentleman. He doesn't push us deeper when we're not ready. He patiently waits to be desired.

⋈⋈

Today, God is calling you deeper
into the river of His Holy Spirit. Dive in!

⋈⋈

The world says to follow your heart. The Word bids us to follow the prompting of the Spirit. What path will you choose today?

⋈⋈

Most devastatingly, the main reason we quench
the Spirit of God is simply because we don't know Him.
He is a stranger to us.

⋈⋈

⋈⋈⋈

We love mountaintops, but our mettle is tested in the devil-prowled desert—where we learn to rely fully on the Holy Spirit.

⋈⋈⋈

We shouldn't seek signs as proof. But the more open we are to the Holy Spirit, the more the power of God will flow through us.

⋈⋈⋈

The power-works of the Holy Spirit are like dynamite,
breaking through the hardest of hearts,
preparing them for the Gospel.

⋈⋈⋈

How far we venture into God's River is up to us. God continues to call, ready to envelop those who choose to go deeper.

⋈⋈⋈

The wonder-working power of Jesus was poured out to
supercharge the testimony of every believer—
through every generation.

We have trouble trusting people to truly manifest the Spirit.
But that's exactly what God does. Even with the least of us.

Intimacy with God requires a leap of faith. We're unsure, wary,
fearful—yet the Spirit still beckons, drawing us deeper.

The Spirit and the Bride really do say, "Come!"
Drink freely of the kingdom's crystal clear, life-giving River.

The Bible is our compass.
If we don't keep confirming our course,
we'll drift off track, far from the current of the Spirit.

The desert is a proving ground, an arid place where we
must learn to rely fully on the refreshment of the Holy Spirit.

The more we're above water, the more control we keep. The
deeper we go into His River, the more control we give to Him.

In the natural we kick back. We take breaks. But the spring
of the Spirit bubbles up eternally for all who would drink.

Healing strikes so deeply
at the core of human need.
It's a phenomenal people magnet,
a powerful gift to be sought.

⋈⋄⋈⋄⋈

Miracles continue today.

There've been storms calmed, blind eyes opened,
food multiplied, deliverance, the dead raised—
all among everyday believers.

⋈⋄⋈⋄⋈

As much as miracles fascinate, most opt to stay in the boat
rather than to step out onto the water in faith as Peter did.
Don't worry what other people think or do.

Follow Jesus.

Our comfort zone is really our control zone.

The more we yield control to Him,
the more comfortable we get with our Comforter.

Spirit-imparted words of knowledge
help us partner with God
to combat lies and speculation
with the undeniable truth
of the Gospel.

Remember Lot's wife.

It's impossible to walk straight ahead while looking back.
Forget the old and move forward
in newness of life.

The manifest gifts are like a set of power tools,
and the gift of faith is like the cord
through which the current flows.

The more we give way to the Holy Spirit, the more His healing
grace flows through us to those who need His touch.

Being called crazy goes with the territory of moving
in the Spirit's power. It happened to Jesus. It'll happen to you.

God won't push us into His River, but He will ask us to trust
Him as He leads beyond the natural into supernatural depths.

When we take our eyes off Jesus,
the power for miracles is broken
and we sink to the limitations
of the natural world.

Though we tend to defer spiritual warfare to leaders,
wolves often attack lone sheep
when earthly shepherds aren't around.

But here's the good news:
The humblest of believers can vanquish the enemy
with a single word: the name of Jesus.

It's not so much about what gift we want (or don't)
as what God wants for us,
what He distributes to each one as He wills.

What kind of person doesn't worry
about what anyone but God thinks?
That would be a person who is truly in love.

Ever the gentleman, our divine Teacher eases us out of our
comfort zones, giving us opportunity to learn about His ways.

If God has spoken to you and yet you find yourself in a pit of
despair like Joseph, look up! Let that pit become a well.

The Bible itself exhorts us to seek modern-day revelation,
every time we're encouraged to listen for God's voice.

It doesn't seem so much a question
of whether or not God is still speaking
as it is whether or not
we are willing to listen.

⁂

We tend to think
God only communicates with shepherds,
but there is one unifying class
to whom He says He speaks:

His sheep.

⁂

Yes. The enemy passes out counterfeit gifts.

But would you throw away real money
just because somebody's printing fakes?

⁂

Hearing God's audible voice commands attention,
but it seems that, more often, He speaks in gentler ways.
Listen for His still, small voice today.

Whereas the voice of our own hearts' desires can easily
disappoint, no word truly spoken by God ever returns void.

God may be using the very hunger and thirst you feel
to draw you away from earthly sustenance and closer to His table.

Reach out when He prompts you. Yield when He subdues you.
Acknowledge Him as your very present helper and guide.

We all have control issues. We like to be in charge of the way
things go. But that is the way of the flesh, not the Spirit.

The pronounced pattern of Scripture
is that God wants to speak to all of His sheep—
to be in vital, personal contact.

Once we truly get to know the Holy Spirit, we'll eagerly accept
what He gives us and we'll go wherever He leads.

Sensitivity to the Holy Spirit is one of the forms discernment
takes, as God reveals the truth about our circumstances.

Sadly, many fear the fire of the Spirit into which Jesus calls us.
They back away, afraid that they'll just get burned.

The same Spirit who burned in Jesus, supernaturally empowering
His ministry, can burn in every single believer today.

If we truly want to be like Jesus,
that means supernatural gifts are standard operating equipment,
even for new believers.

What if our "quiet times" weren't so quiet? What if God spoke to
us, penetrating the silence, just like the Bible promises?

Seeking to be gifted with the word of wisdom?
Don't be surprised if problem-solving ops
start showing up on your doorstep.

If earthly knowledge is power, how much more should we value
super-powered words of knowledge, gifts from the Spirit of God?

When the gift of faith is bestowed, there'll be no doubt,
just the know-that-you-know flow of His power.

The better we get to know God's voice privately, the more easily
we'll be able to hear Him over the din of this world.

We have no power whatsoever in and of ourselves. Zero. One hundred percent of the power to work miracles comes from God.

If it's not done in love, it's not in the Spirit. God's love is more powerful than all the supernatural gifts put together.

If prophecy scares you, you're not alone.
Ask God to speak to you through His Word
and to give you the courage to hear.

Earnest desire to hear God's voice requires us to quiet our human longings, making Him the enduring passion of our souls.

There is more to hear
than is audible to the natural ear.
There's also more to see
than is visible to the natural eye.

When you're ablaze in the Spirit,
people will be drawn to you.

They'll watch you burn
in fascination,
intent upon the flame.

cool waters

✗◇✗

"For with Thee is the fountain of life."

Psalm 36:9b

✗◇✗

Refreshing Currents

If asked what zodiac sign you are,
say you were born under the sign of the cross,
that you follow the Creator of the stars.

Need someone to share the deepest secrets
of your heart with, someone you can truly trust?
Your Father in heaven is a great listener.

When you know the true reason for the season,
it's always Christmas in your heart—
a never-ending celebration of
the continuing Gift of God.

Think of it:

The Author of our faith actively longs for us to find the clues
He's confided through the prophets. He wants us to investigate
symbolic visions and dreams. He waits for us to dig deep
and unearth the secret treasures that those who seek Him
with all their hearts are rewarded to discover.

Give extravagant grace today,
beyond what anyone could ever ask or think.
Echo the kind of favor God lavishes on us.

No matter the price,
living in the Truth
is more than worth it.
The benefits are literally endless.

There is no greater gift
than the One given
to the whole world:
wrapped in love,
sealed with hope,
found not under a tree,
but upon one.

Thank God for the challenging people in your life.
They are instruments God uses to shape you
into His forgiving, compassionate image.

There's no need to strive with others
to facilitate God's will.
Trust that God hears your prayers.
Know that the way of the Spirit is peace.

The sharing of secrets is a privilege of intimate relationship.
That's exactly the kind of closeness God wants with His people.
He'll give us understanding of life's mysteries
when we sit at His feet.
What is hidden will be brought to light.
Understanding will grow as we get to know Him better,
in that secret place of fellowship with Him.

༺༻

Are you hurting?

Our Great Physician knows what it is to live
with chronic pain better than anyone.

He can be a balm to your wounds.

༺༻

Be generous with your smile.
Give that good medicine that a cheerful heart can be,
no matter your circumstance.

༺༻

We think we can't make it,
that we can't go another step.

But what better time to let go and let
God be the hero to us that He is?

༺༻

Why wish on a star (or a dandelion),
when you can talk to the One who made them?

Listen with spiritual ears.
You might just hear that still, small voice of God,
speaking to you, just like He promised.

There is plenty of time in every day
to do everything God wants you to do.

There is such hope in Christmas. Not Santa. Not presents.
Not mistletoe and holly. The real deal. Best re-giftable gift ever.

When it comes to finding godly contentment,
it's not so much a question of *where* we are as it is *who* has led us
to that place. If God led you into that valley, thank Him for it.
He will strengthen you to not only survive it, but also to thrive.

Wherever you are, there is a Fountain.

Truly.

⸻

God cares about the intricacies of your life.
Don't hesitate to talk to Him about anything.
If it matters to you, it matters to Him.

⸻

Don't fret when others receive blessings you don't.
God sees you and knows what's truly best for you.
It's about much more than this life.

Good news:

We don't have to wait for the physical resurrection of the dead to start living in the kingdom. Jesus said the kingdom is at hand. The spiritually dry and dead can be resurrected at any time—
in a moment—starting in the here and now.
It's a message of hope God has hidden in our hearts,
embedded with a call to be messengers for Him.

Pray before you act. Listen before you speak.
Your heavenly Counselor will guide you, if given the opportunity.
All heaven can break loose.

If we only find pleasure in reaping,
we miss the joys of sowing, tending, and watering.
Every step can be bliss.

We aren't really free
until we're unchained
from the slavery
of what people think of us.

God's perspective is the only one that matters.

Choice by choice,
each new day brings opportunity
to deny the flesh, yield to the Spirit,
and allow God's refreshing grace
to flow.

The virtue of goodness is often under-appreciated
till evil threatens. It's the fruit of the Spirit—
sweet refuge within life's storms.

Desire interaction with God?

He desires it with you.
Ask Him a sincere question,
then listen for the answer through the day.

If you're having trouble understanding
something in the Bible, ask God to explain it to you.

He invites you to reason and interact with Him.

Before you get into trending:

Think carefully about who you're following.
Trending can be good or bad,
depending on who leads the way.

Inquire of the Lord
before making and carrying out your plans.
Ask if that trip, commitment, or job is in
His perfect plans for you.

This is God's day.
Rain or shine, it's always His,
but notice it especially today since it's just like He is:
gorgeous beyond expression.

Spend time in quietness,
with your ears open
to the Holy Spirit.
In those silent moments,
you just may hear
His whispers.

True peace is not disturbed by circumstances.
It rests, comfortably assured in the Savior's arms,
in the midst of life's storms.

Feel like you're spinning your wheels?

There might be something
God is trying to get through to you
before He'll let you progress.

Unsure what to do?

Ask your heavenly Father's advice.
Sit at His feet and listen.
He loves that.
He delights to answer and help His kids.

⋈⋈

No matter what happens,
God can use it in His children's lives,
along His continuum of redemption and grace.

It really is all good.

⋈⋈

Savor a day of rest.

There is plenty of time
for work six days a week.
God knows a break from our labors
refreshes us for the week to come.

⋈⋈

No matter how challenging,
every day is a gift.
Every single day.

⋈⋈

When was the last time
you introduced yourself to a total stranger?
It can be life-changing.
Just ask the woman at the well.

Worship is more than simply going to church.
It is a responsive awareness of the presence of God,
wherever we are,
every day of the week.

Wherever you go,
leave a trail of light.
Illuminate the world.

liquid love

✕✕✕

*"He will rejoice over you with joy,
He will be quiet in His love,
He will rejoice over your with shouts of joy."*

Zephaniah 3:17

✕✕✕

Awash in Adoration

have *Faith* despite your yesterdays

Hope for today

and *Love* like there's no tomorrow.

~susan rohrer

Have faith despite your yesterdays.
Hope for today.
Love like there's no tomorrow.

No one is beyond the scope of God's love and power.
Never give up on that loved one.
As long as there is breath, there is hope.

Express your love for someone today. In words or deeds,
say what every person longs to hear: that they matter to you.

Every day is a new opportunity to love
and serve the God who first loved and served us.

Start this day with God. Live this day in love. End this day
knowing the soul-level peace that comes with eternal security.

LIQUID LOVE: AWASH IN ADORATION

※※※

There is no end to the love of our Father God.
It endures through our unfaithful wanderings,
waiting patiently for us to come home.

※※※

Forgive those who have wronged you.
Love and pray for them with all your heart.
Freely give them the undeserved favor
God has given to you.

※※※

In a pressure cooker?

Release your anxiety to God.
Talk it out;
cry it out.
Let Him lead you to still waters
by His loving hand.

※※※

Jesus constantly talks to the Father on our behalf,
advocating for us, knowing our every need.
His desire is always to embrace us in His tender compassion,
to bind up our broken hearts,
to water our dry bones with His Word,
to restore the breath of His Spirit into our lungs,
and to resurrect us to the glories of abundant life.

God's love doesn't restrict us
from anything that is truly good for us.
When God says *no* or *don't*,
it is with our very best at heart.

Love your enemies in word and deed.
Go deeper than the letter of the law of love
to the grace-giving, self-sacrificing Spirit of it.

LIQUID LOVE: AWASH IN ADORATION

⋈

Love the Lord with all your soul, that deep-set center of your will.
Let earthly desires fade in the light of your desire to please Him.

⋈

The world loves us when we are at our best,
but God loves us when we are at our worst.
Be a vessel of grace to someone who needs it today.

⋈

Don't you just love the quiet of the morning?
It's the perfect time to hear God's still, small voice.

⋈

Loving the work God sets before us makes our labors much
more of a smile than a groan. If you have a job, be thankful.

⋈

Love.

Even when you are rejected,
scorned, or ignored.
Love bears all of these things
and keeps on giving.

⋈⋈

Bottom line:
It really is all about relationship.
It's about discovering true love and refreshment,
in the arms of the Lover of our souls.

thirst quenchers

※◇◇◇※

"But whoever drinks of the water that I shall give him shall never thirst; but the water that I shall give him shall become in him a well of water springing up to eternal life."

John 4:14

※◇◇◇※

Hydration for Dry Days

THIRST QUENCHERS: HYDRATION FOR DRY DAYS

Need a refill?

The crystal clear waters of the Holy Spirit
are available to all who believe.
It is His joy to refresh the thirsty.
Ask for an outpouring today.

Practice gratitude for all God is doing,
even though you can't see it.
When things seem still,
trust that your invisible Advocate is moving.

Every morning, wake up
and, no matter what, try and say:

"Thank you for this day.
The past, it's behind me.
New mercies are ahead."

Godly character isn't birthed out of ease.
It is built on hardship and refined by suffering.

It is the sweet fruit of His Spirit in you.

⨯⬦⨯

Correction can sting,
but what a gift it is to know
what we can improve upon and fix.

⨯⬦⨯

The antidote for boredom is life in the Spirit.
There is always something interesting to do.

⨯⬦⨯

Speak words of grace. Filter every thought through the wisdom
and kindness of the Holy Spirit, before you give it utterance.

⨯⬦⨯

God is not finished with you. There's no winding down with age.
Check Proverbs 15:24 and see: the wise wind up!

⨯⬦⨯

Be diligent
as you go about your work
and trust God for the timing.
Fruit needs time in the sun to ripen.

There is always a reason to give thanks—
for what we've already been given,
for what we enjoy now,
and for all the grace
that is to come.

House cleaning?

Start in the recesses of your heart,
the temple of the Holy Spirit.
You'll find a willing Helper.

If your faith is barely flickering,
your hope down to an ember,
ask God to blow on it.
You can trust Him to be gentle
as He feeds the flame.

⁂

Don't fret about how things look.
God is working in the invisible realm
for the good of all those who trust Him.

⁂

We begin to age gracefully
when we become
more grateful to God
for the number of candles
on our birthday cakes
than we are ashamed of them.

God's peace is available to you
in the midst of life's storms.
No matter how fierce the gale,
He is an ever-present anchor to your soul.

We may feel like we've blown it for good,
like we're unlovable messes.
But forever and always, God is for us,
longing for the day when we turn from our ways
and head for the comforts of home.

There is always the temptation
to draw old wine out of old wineskins,
from what is familiar.
Ask for new wine today.
It will be much better.

If you're feeling dry,
just like the woman at the well,
you need the wellspring of the Spirit.
Drink of that water
and you needn't ever be parched again.

There's a reason that the sword of the Spirit
is the only offensive equipment in the armor of God.

The weapons of our warfare are spiritual.

Aren't you glad His mercies
are new every morning?
That means we can start fresh,
with a clean slate,
every single day.

Don't hesitate to seek godly counsel.

It is a courageous act
to lay your struggles bare
in the company of those who can offer wisdom to you.

Abide in Him.
Live in that dwelling place of peace,
no matter what tempts you to move.

It can be truly challenging
when God says: "Wait."

But He knows we need time
for the fruit of patience to mature
in our ever-wanting hearts.

Balaam's donkey is a good reminder that the obstacles we rail at may actually be put there by God, slowing us down with purpose.

A valley can be a lush, fruitful place
as long as we are watered by the Holy Spirit.
We can be like those trees Ezekiel talks about,
in the valley below the cliffs of Engedi.
Year-round, we can bear fruit
if we're drinking from God's river.
(Ezekiel 47:12)

It's easy to obey God
when it seems to benefit us.
But we need to grasp that it's always
for our good to obey Him,
even when it seems hard.

When things are difficult to understand,
ask the Holy Spirit to explain what the Bible has to say.
He patiently teaches those who'll listen.

No matter how complex the problem,
God has a solution.

Sit at His feet.
He has all the wisdom you need
to rightly navigate every challenge.

Not hearing from heaven?

God may be waiting for you
to respond to what He's already spoken.
Ask if there's a backlog awaiting attention.

No matter the place you find yourself, know that
God sees you there. Like the loving Father that He is,
He cares about your mountaintops and your valleys.
Wherever you are, you are never, ever, out of His sight.
He waits to water your dry bones and to restore you to
a place of spiritual vitality in every single circumstance.

God really does have all the answers.
The greatest enigmas are elegantly solved
at the feet of such a Teacher.

Today is a golden opportunity
to put the past behind
and walk forward in newness of life.
Forget what has been forgiven.
Onward in faith.

Feeling hopeless?

Having a hard time feeling at home in that valley? Take heart.
This world is not our home. Heaven is. Forever.
What a bright and glorious hope Christ freely gives,
to all who would dare to believe.

Peace is not the absence of tribulation.
It is the unshakeable assurance that God is with us
in the midst of life's storms.

You are a new creation.

Why crawl in the dirt of your old life
when God has equipped you so beautifully
to take to the skies?

swimming single

>≈<>≈<

*"Delight yourself in the Lord;
and He will give you the desires of your heart."*

Psalm 37:4

>≈<>≈<

Lifelines for Spouse Seekers

> True love is patient. God's best is always worth the wait.
>
> ~ susan rohrer
> IS GOD SAYING HE'S THE ONE?

True love is patient. God's best is always worth the wait.

><><><

The most romantic thing a man can do
is to bear the fruit of the Spirit:
love, joy, peace, patience, gentleness,
self-control, goodness, humility, and faith.

><><><

There's no need to obsess over if, when, or where
a particular place of intersection will come to be.
If two people who are meant to marry are following God,
He'll arrange for them to find each other
somewhere along the way.

Marriage is a covenant relationship and God is a covenant keeper.
He is the essence of faithfulness, so He doesn't encourage
His children to be unfaithful in any way, shape, or form.

Choose life, Daughter of God.

Choose the man God is saying He wants for you—a man whose character is fashioned by grace. Choose a man who will love you like Christ loves the Church, a man who is willing to lay down the very life God gives him for the sake of his cherished bride.

Is that man bitter or sweet? You can tell what kind of fruit is in a man by what comes out when someone gives him a hard squeeze.

⁂

Just as hunger prompts us to eat and thirst make us want something to drink, time without committed companionship draws us to desire each other. Resist the appetites of the flesh and give way to the Spirit.

⁂

Truth in love, Sisters:

You can't help it. You play house, instinctively.
Just like a sparrow is hard-wired to build her nest,
your soulful heart will automatically begin to gather twigs
when you spend time with a man you find to be attractive.
Every date, every call or text, every expression of affection
adds to the growing framework. That's why it's never just a date.

⁂

As much as we can tend to treat Him otherwise, the Holy Spirit doesn't operate like a love potion. No matter how much you plead, beg, bargain, or cajole, God will not force a man to choose you. There's a very good reason for that. God knows you will be better off with a man who chooses you of his own accord.

Just as God longs to be desired for Himself, He understands that you need more than a half-hearted man who has been talked into choosing you or pushed in your direction.

Truth in love, Sisters:

As good as it feels to have those regular calls, to get those funny texts, or even to just see his face—if you want commitment and he doesn't, you're hurting yourself every single time you perpetuate the pattern.

>◇◇◇<

While spiritual adornment reveals the truth of the heart, earthly clothing covers. It hides what's really underneath. Contrary to conventional wisdom, not every man is what he wears.

>◇◇◇<

If you're marriage-minded and he isn't—you're unequally yoked. You're committed romantically, but he's not. If your heart is ever to get to the place where you are ready to be married to another man, one day, you'll have to get over this one.

>◇◇◇<

Do not accept a man's proposal until you have successfully worked through at least one significant disagreement, better yet a heated argument that leaves at least one of you (preferably both) in tears. You may say you're in love, that you get along famously, and that you never fight. But if you've never been in the thick of serious conflict resolution with that man, you don't really know him.

>◇◇◇<

Does God speak
to the choice of a husband?

As the heavenly Father of the bride,
it does seem like
He'd have an opinion.

Know this:

If he's a guy that God
is suggesting as a good choice for you,
he is a man who talks to God.
He's a man who listens
for what God might say back to him,
even about the choice of a spouse.
He's a man who would be willing to pray
about what place you might hold in his life.
He is also man enough
to be honest with you
about how he feels.

The more you resist the flesh
and give way to the Spirit,
the sharper your ears will be
to hear what God is saying to you
about that special man in your life.

⋈⋄⋈

The key to finding The One?

It's about being in the center of God's will,
that place where God knows you'll meet up
with all that He has planned for you.

⋈⋄⋈

No matter your earthly marital status,
know that in God's eyes you are chosen.
He is your divine husband. The Lover of your soul.
And you are His cherished, beautiful bride.

⋈⋄⋈

afterword

><><><>

Jesus cried out and said, "He who believes in Me, as the Scripture said, 'From out of his innermost being shall flow rivers of living water.'" But this He spoke of the Spirit, whom those who believed in Him were to receive.

John 7:3

One of the things I love so much about the invitation God extends is that it's to everyone. There's no exclusivity of gender, race, or age. All who live and breathe are invited into His sparkling river.

It's been many years since I answered His invitation at almost seventeen. I didn't know what a radical change of course it would be, or how powerfully those rivers would flow. I didn't realize how profoundly I'd come to adore and depend upon Him. I'd just met someone who had what I didn't have, what I wanted: soul deep security, peace, joy, and love.

Suddenly, it all became very simple to put aside who I was and receive what only God could give me. I'd done nothing to work my way into His favor. It didn't matter that I accepted God's invitation while sitting in the back seat of a parked car with my friend. Jesus met me where I was that day, and I have never been the same.

It really was just as He promised. As soon as I opened the door to Him, those rivers began to flow—cleansing me through and through—carrying me on His current of grace. Even when I fall short.

Decades have come and gone, and those waters continue to wash and renew me day-to-day, moment-by-moment. If you've accepted His invitation, too, you know what I mean. But if you haven't yet—or if you've wandered away from His life-giving flow, know that your forgiving God stands waiting, loving you all the while.

Not another minute has to pass before you embark on this journey of faith. You can accept His invitation right now. It's fine if you'd like to use your own words. Or if you're unsure what to say, you can pray this prayer with me:

My Lord and my God,

How wonderful You are to invite me into relationship with You. To shower me with such grace. Thank You for forgiving me and washing me clean. I believe that You loved me so much that You gave your only Son to die for me. Even now, You're resurrecting me with Him, and giving me new life.

Please tend this seed of faith you've given me. Help me to grow. Right now, I open myself to receive your Holy Spirit. Release those rivers of living water from within me. Let this be the first day of my eternal life with You.

I ask all of this in the name of Jesus. Amen.

AFTERWORD

If you just prayed that prayer with me, welcome to the family of God. It's always exciting to have new brothers and sisters splashing in His river. I hope you'll drink deep of the fresh water He offers in limitless supply.

To get off to a good start, may I suggest a few ways to stay in the flow? Find a vibrant, believing church and introduce yourself. Ask if they have a small group to nurture new believers. Allow God to water you by reading *the Bible*, starting in the New Testament with *the Gospel of John*. Ask the Holy Spirit to help you understand what He's saying to you with each passage. Feel free to pose questions and listen for His answers. Let that conversation continue throughout the day. Pretty soon you'll sense a divine friendship growing, one you can rely on for eternity.

about the author

SUSAN ROHRER enjoys wearing a wide variety of professional hats. A professional writer, producer, and director specializing in redemptive entertainment, her screen credits in one or more of these capacities include: *God's Trombones; Another Life;* Humanitas Prize finalist & Emmy winner *Never Say Goodbye;* Emmy nominees *Terrible Things My Mother Told Me* and *The Emancipation of Lizzie Stern; No Earthly Reason;* NAACP Image Award nominated film: *Mother's Day;* AWRT Public Service Award winner *Sexual Considerations* (for addressing the problem of teen sexual harassment); telefilms *Book of Days* and *Another Pretty Face;* Emmy *Considerations; Sweet Valley High;* nominee & Humanitas Prize finalist *If I Die Before I Wake;* as well as Film Advisory Board & Christopher Award winner: *About Sarah.*

In addition to authoring a number of inspirational nonfiction books, Rohrer is also the author of several novels in the Redeeming Romance Series, based on her original screenplays.

REDEEMING ROMANCES BY SUSAN ROHRER

NONFICTION BY SUSAN ROHRER

A Final Note
Before We Say Goodbye

⋈⋈

Dear Reader,

Thanks so much for the time we've spent together as you've read this collection of inspirational quotations. I hope you found personal application and encouragement in these pages.

Would you consider posting a quick review? It's easy. Just go to this book's page on Amazon. You'll get to share your reading experience with family, friends, as well as other readers across the world, and I'll truly appreciate your feedback.

Gratefully,
Susan Rohrer